# INCLINED

## TO RIOT

Sibling Rivalry Press, LLC
PO Box 26147
Little Rock, AR 72221

info@siblingrivalrypress.com

www.siblingrivalrypress.com

ISBN: 978-1-943977-58-1

Library of Congress Control No: 2018960662

By special invitation, this title is housed in the Rare Book and Special Collections Vault of the Library of Congress.

First Sibling Rivalry Press Edition, May 2019

# INCLINED
## TO RIOT

## KMA
# SULLIVAN

**SIBLING RIVALRY PRESS**

DISTURB / ENRAPTURE

LITTLE ROCK / ARKANSAS

# contents

## this is how I dress my face

a bit of shine and dark at the eye
enough to look like I'm paying attention
this is how I see you fresh
wingtips and socks to the knee
the hole between skin and self spreading
I used to sink into your sounds
there was comfort there guttural and soft
but that was before you asked
me to spin on a pole
while you hummed in the neon
as the night came down
this is how I leave you
climbing granite stairs
dragging my pieces at the ankle
who can know the tangle of hands and hair
the forests heavy with moss and dream
two limbless creatures can sing themselves into life
and lose
today eyes are drawn on my lids
and that's enough seeing
you won't catch my eyes unpainted again

## willing absence

things that are true
rarely behave
my mind races itself
like a lawn windmill
with arms spinning
forever staked to the ground
or the brass rooster
on the barn roof
no one ever thinks he will fly
find his patch of seed
his perfect hen or cock
in the morning
my red socks hit the pine floor
track debris
bits of typewriter ribbon
and pomegranate
with leaf tongue
I lick the air
taste what is new
you were an unexpected moment
and kept me safe from myself for a while
but what I thought were luminous currents
now feel more like knitting patterns
this life is a smoking gyre

step away
if you don't want
to spin and burn

## rain on wheat field

is all I can see from this room
water cuts sky and ground
all these nude women
these large bathers
I don't wait
for the moon to shine
but flowers by picasso
are still a surprise
I guess we can all be pedestrian
careful man
so boneless are your edges
stretched and coming
the smallest polished haunch
at once grotesque and romantic
my legs dangle at the drain
unshaven without knees
made of beeswax and human hair
legs in lieu of faucet
I smell your brain case
all aluminum tabs and potting soil
I am over you

## in certain valleys

there is a hare in the forest
a clump of lady's mantle
I will eat with you eat you
on this curved surface
eyebrow sprouting
but the seraphim are in pieces
even with a donkey at my feet
and a blue tiled floor
I am bewildered
dropping clothes
running
can we not choose happiness
a white bird with outstretched wings
european woods and porphyry?
I keep my mace close
like my heart it is blue bulging
I refuse to be owned by desire
live in a cage of my own making
or yours
this beauty is on loan
the rest
a toothless spotted horse

## embrace the marvelous

the open spatial fields
these private obsessions
where blood flows from keyholes
while the billiard table offers a palette
of sound and movement
among gelded sacraments
let's aim for the hole
so we might spring from the corner
and collapse back in
heart and genitals descending
the cubists got it right
we are all this fractured form
but we make it down the stairs
with our pieces tumbling
choose among milkmaid and saint
and slotted spoon
there are pills strung on a wire
fear in the meaningless chatter
for love I might burn off my fingerprints
an elaborate detour toward a blameless life
the pig glances sideways
from the watering trough
she knows better

## inveterate traveler

for all your tall trees
we still play hide and seek
in the shadow of skirted pines
as we climb to your high pasture
the clouds flower
the clouds yawn and devour
snow buttercup will not sustain
the sheep on these rocks
their hunger is a revelation
even the landscape is in mourning
but these are not my mountains and fields
my smoke
my fingered sky
like the snow buttercup I will follow the sun
this time down the mountain
so I stand here
embroidered skirts shifting in the breeze
pitchfork sparkling
though perhaps it is a divining rod
how many days of rain
do we inherit
of those how many do we ignore
or push past?

I might yet smell the river
even the fish have faces here
I am ready to build mine

## temple interior

shrine dancer
ring on my thumb
fabric pops
to a frivolous tune
erotic
untitled
there are crows in every cherry tree
lord of obstacles
it is my belly
that contains the universe
you ask for babies
who emerge pristine
prussian blue
but there is so much to carry
across this bridge
where are the festivals?
all I see is tiny fires
that bloom from armchairs
and cut fruit
a paragon of composure
is what you desire
fuck you

## light box

since no two moments are the same
I decide to cut a carpenter's pencil
or maybe I'll watch
the movement of green
thread and balloon flowers
a seed pod
I'd like a tomorrow without constraints
the grace of insect architecture
a paper wasp nest
so much becomes clear from a distance
why do I press my face to the glass?
I pray I will be faithful
but coffee spills over my pants
like a mechanical arm reaching for a purple rabbit
I insist on my right to exist
with or without a baseball bat
a repurposed machine

## knee deep

rice and roots in hand
heavy and caked
I didn't count on the mud
demanding
I bend at the waist
there is a chronicle of grief
eroded ground and ash boiling
if you get close enough
even the fig writhes within itself
but every now and then
I think of you
of us fumbling
there is no grace in confused hearts
each of us stumbling
remembering promises we've made
these alternate currents
won't deliver us to a coral reef
with all its blues on the surface
and anemone below
but perhaps to a delta
that has flowed for so long
its edges are flat
there is wandering in the silt
water and earth almost the same

## ambivalence

bottles and frogs
a moustache floating
I am in flux
a hinge
matisse's lemons
his lutes and platters
props all freely lifted
I wrap them in my hair
I peel back skin
call myself carmelina
add touches of graphite
to my winding paths
miró's birds are indifferent
increasingly attenuated
my mouth becomes the wall
becomes the book
becomes my face and thumbs emerging
who needs arms
the hole is the thing

## rosewood zither

add strings to change volume
shading of pitch
you are the musician
press my fretted fingerboard
the crocodile's hum
offers a slow unfolding
pluck me
you can be my bamboo flute
my mouth will find you
you can be my rin gong
my medicine bowl
with ring and mallet
I will make you sing
in tibet there are trumpets made of bone
human or tiger
fitted with brass and leather
a mouth-piece
vibrations dissolve flesh and self
place my bones in a basket
I will sound for you and disappear

## special exhibit

rock head
collected hair
I see myself in planks
and plastic trees
coffee pots
bold and boundless
scrape the sky
there is temporary flair
a dress with a window
who decides
what is worth preserving?
I cast my mother's hand
her mouth
in silver
but remain a wing nut
a wash
stained and hovering
I don't know why I love you
looping skeins
a gesture
I curl into your scattering

## american line

her marbled body
a jack-in-the-pulpit
with tongue at the top
sits here for him
the harlequin musician
hat and eyelashes
he offers a house in the suburbs
all fish and line
all window and clock
oh to have so many improvisations
they need to be numbered
like kandinsky
a sea battle
with pink sails
but instead just a clay head
cheeks and chin
same as hair
she is a bird
a helmeted warrior
a cabbage
he will beguile her
with van gogh
and those green babies

## red light on egyptian blue

granite arm broken off
laid beside
the colossal head
a fragment of beard
a sphinx
I'll attend
to even the smallest bit
of worn wisdom
or painted grace
there, a false door
I will sit in its frame
with my own lion face
paws draped
in bracelets and sunflowers
I place feathers
in the curls
of your beard
*I will pull your chariot* you say
but even if you give me
a beaded raven head
place gold wires at my neck
a cut for each accomplishment
you will not reach my high city
nor see my luminescence

# boating party

who paints the sulfur
muck that will suck me
to the hip
dragonfly
in the yellow
tranquil encounter
leaves circling
beneath tongue mountain
there are marshes
meticulous and wild
no pink clouds at sunset
instead there is a mill
a footbridge
nearly invisible
this is not my niagara
but even ponds crest
dressed in pink tulle
pink down to the feathers
of my fan
not merely in fabric
I froth for you

## inclined to riot

I am there in the white
between socket and smudge
I will strip you down to the shaker
salt every tooth
I am interested
but I do not love you
with the weight of these strange cushions
enormous and sagging
I could sink you sink
into you sink you
leave hand prints and burning
on your spleen
not the normal splatter and drip
a fresh cunt spitting
I will clean my teeth with your ardor
a treat in the toothpaste
there is a version of myself
fragile and alert
intentional trash
a cool touch might teach me
jesus I want to yell
cover myself in folded paper
and half an idea
have a tantrum in the flowers
BAD DOG

## still life

roast duck and joint meats
shaped loaves and red grapes
I am roughly ground
a mummified bull
wheels cut into my chest
you will hunt in my brine marsh
take a small boat
a knife
but you will not find me
among the coniferous soft woods
I can hide
in the twisted winter bark
of blueberry trees
even when you fill my canopic jars
secure my fingernails and skin
with thread
place a garland of twisted copper
over my eyes
sure
I believe in happiness
this death mask

## postmodern

I wonder how long
it is going to take
to be free of you
light echoes and envelops
and organizes space
there is an instinctive grasp
of fractals, nature's patterns
an existential unease
rothko's color blocks
brick me in
while outside birds are pinned
to the sky
I thought I would soar
even after the pork-butcher babies came
resembling and reassembled
I built a ramshackle house
scraped and painted over
earlier histories
my younger self
feather earrings and tasseled skirts
squeegee my face

## my breasts have been full for you

suck as you will
stone boat
I will tell you about the fisherman
consorting with the crocodiles
have I thrown the net
or been hooked at the mouth?
a lost tomb
I want a pool full of birds
bordered by jasmine
shaded by sycamore figs and date palms
I will fill my spaces
with lotus blossoms
and plain tiger butterflies
scale and shine
lay me out full
I want this painted coffin
to be long
take up space

## processional of the moon

along this arcaded walkway
I think of ancient things
cleopatra, elgin marbles, my body
like an egyptian priest
you bleed, gut and bind me
liver, lungs, intestines
packed comfortably in canopic jars
I thought conjugal bliss
meant cloisonné and jade rings
latticed doors
twelve cypress posts
to support the roof
there would be evanescent joys
shades of fawn and umber
among persian tile
I, your pillared temple
you, my recumbent knight
instead I think about statues
of the dead
seek the second book of breathing
long for a sandstone cocoon

## secret threshing

I walk your landscape
with its tightly budded trees
your lack of charity
and wealth of hurdy-gurdies
render you exotic
but not long suffering
while I am a bactrian camel
in search of a tavern, a turnstile, the rhine
I am fascinated by hybrid creatures
ostrich plumes, trolls
so I let you print me in stages
sugar lift
aqua tint
waiting for the acid to bite
I am catlicked
wondering when dürer's lions will consume me
or perhaps inkless today
you press in
I am embossed
your anonymous mother
your 17<sup>th</sup> century prostitute

## so careful these edges

oh jumbled color and flush
my favorite nightgown
your smoldering black
so many galaxies abandoned
there is collision and detour
a mad dog
tits to cunt
you will sink me
in pink marble
with christ's blessing
and a window grille
ring my head with ash
all these suspended stars
nailed and dripping
how best can I show you
bird-man?
all I want is a walnut cradle
detail in the carving
three faces and a rope
mirrored and mounted
I am that ancient swinging door

# here

a glass box of broken limbs
face worn away
I can still ride this horse
glow at night
like red light on egyptian blue
I was born to be luminescent
a stampede
here
forced down on one knee
held by my hair
that languid boy
cast a shadow even in relief
even in fragments
mouth open, nostrils flared
I am nomad, moon goddess, carbon smear
if wings sprouted from my face
I would not fly back

## expressionist interior

even distorted
one can find my belly,
breasts, the point
where men enter
sonorous color
tell me that I am more
than a carrier of men
giacometti shadows
women into birthday candles
precarious and absurd
with large feet
and eroded heart
I burn for boys' wishes
poetry, that wild beast
could take what is left
epoxy resin and marble dust
mix the paste
start again

## the christ child so strange

in those early florentine oils
green skin and odd smile
as in fra angelico's *adoration*
you place gold at my feet
oh the flamboyance of men
how they love to show their tail feathers
like a pheasant diving off a roof
toward a lady much admired
who sits before juniper
and a wax seal
men say she is unfinished
but who decides?
there is dirt at her neck and mouth
in spite of the pearls
oh the fucking
and feeding of parrots
I am so tired of pretty women
who lay themselves out in marble
and blown lace
but there is a dog
in the timothy grass
a figure barely visible and waiting
no wonder we recline on couches

## french color theory

men and women stop
at the enameled orchid brooch
tremblers in the case
and out
who cannot resist
vitreous mouth
slick
petals streaked with red
the diamond heart
denying space
refusing shadow
monet offers little depth
colors swirl
not as objects in relation
but water lilies and willows
as one
a landscape moving inside itself
I wait for your tongue
to leave me
slick and trembling

## porcelain for the emperor

elegant woman
there is artless style
you are phoenix
a traveling foundry
burn me
what key will unlock this ceramic box?
must it have tines?
in el greco there is ecstasy
light held in the folds
christ a pink landmass
even roughly sketched I can see
the rhythm of you
your planes
your red flower
this is the thickthin of it
this is the leftright of it
you are my enameled rose
my fruit dish
but I can't decide if your hole
is a green pear on a plate
or a bloody hand print

## verisimilitude

saint catherine was sad
even before
she was strapped to a wheel
by the man who promised
to love her
she held the martyr's palm
lizzie boott was so loved
she was covered
in marble folds and fronds
horses spring from the walls
there's a girl
with a sickle at her waist
she braids straw
waits for the cutting
in bright colors and broken brush work
her delicate shoes
the ribbons
she dares to be empty
even if you splash water
over her colored shadows
you will not know her
she balances
skirt out
watches and keys hanging

on satin cord
she will show you her pearl collar
but she will not close her eyes

## pomegranates and pinecones

stone rosettes at the doorway
an italian marriage chest
be careful maiden
the forest might eviscerate
better the walnut sarcophagus
proserpina has time
spring with her mother
and winter underground
brocade screens
for style and status
small capitals and thick foliage
carved into a stone fireplace
in the book of hours
there are prayers
secular scribes
illustrators
ink and parchment makers
devoted to the virgin
her white breasts
offer aids to meditation
two fingers up
for benediction on that silvered hand
with hair down to the grass
my toes dig through

a window into my remains
I am a living reliquary
a fantastic dragon

## origin story

with flour up to my elbows
I seek false indigo
and the creeping fig
dodge desiccating winds
that leave only spine and hair
we are numbered
covered in fringe
and our universes
I may yet find
the asparagus flower
a peppermint scented geranium
you are my yoked bull
bowls of corn and seed
your blood becomes silver
my heart becomes peyote
we will dig rivers with this glass plow

# chihuly

bowls of orange and yellow
shout happiness
flowers spring from one another
in the folded glowing
more beautiful in shadow and mirror
they show their serious side
with a missing eye
a useless arm
he forced a new way
found a scarlet chandelier
and my transparencies
gravity
movement
centrifugal force
swim through lilac streaked air
my arms curl
to grasp desire
but this playground
remains
a perfect stillness

## there is a garden filled with debris

where the peace of the acorns
and moving water
the sound of the flowers
resting among dragon medallions
and random limbs
announces that it is time to ask
how much has been stolen
there is a headless statue
in the hydrangea and palm
see how she bends at the elbow
as if she still carries
what might make a difference
once there were blown glass beads
an exuberant fountain
she celebrated each peony
the soft simplicity of growing things
little is meant to become new again
but this villa with its matted gardens
where young wanderers pose
snap photos
laugh at what is missed
calls itself a castle
is that what happens when the periphery darkens?
we imagine ourselves grander

even as we diminish
the light moves inside
surrounded by what is broken
by the pieces that will not mend
we glow

## burying ground

it was a perfect miracle
with ointments and scarves
secrets resting in piles
who would know me tied to bed posts
loosely
but still
while you illicit pathos from the barista
does she know you left the breasts of your ex
black with bruising
that you wanted to fuck her unconscious
and have her wake to your fists?
sweater vests end up weak storytellers
the buttons cover holes in your chest
you were a bright minute
but your form
no longer fresh
smells of burnt coffee
and towels that won't wash themselves
you think this is the game
it isn't even the warm-up

# the city endures

wrecking ball pulses
through brick and shadow
counting frailties
the backslide of man
in the sensorium
there is a palpable sense of menace
when will I learn
to interrogate desire
notice what emerges at low tide
what is waiting to rise
there is tar on the wall
genitals in chalk and concrete
a ceaseless obsolescence
so old
I'm almost in the trash
with large sunglasses
and mannequin hands
you might have your numbered flags
your banded hats and guns
but I have a fetish for novelty
minute particulars
in triangular spaces
where there is dimensionality
even in the dappling

so I will lurch out of subway cars
knock into tall women
newly minted
be happy just
to balance on heel bone
even as the boa constrictor
approaches the playpen

## what is life but a pout and a missing tooth?

I will rest on this anchor
with its houseboat and tin awning
there is a lack of bridges
no fire escapes into the water
just blurred reflection
as we grow on each other's leashes
and fuck what legs we can find
sometimes we miss the bone
and can't tell if what's before us
is a scaffold or a drunkard's path
but this is the time for language
and its curbside garbage
like a waterfall
projected on glass
the rush and pound of it
even on the floor
even on the wall
I want to get to the YES
set the price for catching up
but I'm in the wrong gallery
for this lifted eye

## seated woman are you done at 54?

no words
just face and shadow
idealized woman
particularized man
with a nose like a knife
and hair alive with serpents
I strain the sugar
move from green to glow
so I can find the lightning
this variant state
with its special spoons
the lives that hold us together
as we pull into ourselves
pull each other apart
I hold up a mirror
but refuse to look
as grasses spring from my thigh
the sturdiest part of me
the now and arrow of me
my head a painted sieve
once held lettuce and green beans
caught water
let it go
I am simultaneously

female and phallic
luminous white plaster
to mold and carve
nose and crown
with all four fingers
I work in haste
and defiance

## armature

feet and claws and elegant shoes
toes pointed out
my ass a shovel
here is my swirling face
with twisted painted neck
and a crown of nails
I will work on one part today
one facet
one plane
leave the rest for you to wonder
why women reading are decoration
we don't need heads
just hands
just breasts
bellies
a cunt
strap my feet to the floor
if you walk to the left
my face disappears
and you will begin to see my feathers
what you choose to polish
udder
teet and clit
what a man might fondle

might enter
the bull and all his parts
he photographs with more power
and space
than he lives
in life he is more palm frond
with various branches
rodin offers joan of arc
her head of sorrow
in ecstasy
among twigs on fire
I refuse to sit for my portrait
become a placeholder
a fragment of a door

## how relaxing it is to concentrate on one's foot

in caravaggio light is a mask
it points to what we don't know
shows us that we don't know it
rembrandt is so dark
he pulls us in
so we might see the small flame
while goya finds beauty in black lace
and an uneven eye
wrists covered
fingers curved touching
a fan
we enjoy amorous approaches
or hold a lover at bay
sometimes these look the same
sargent pushes our fire out
we glow at skirt and neck
the position of head
he sees us in the shadows
what we keep inside
the quiet contentment in botticelli
what he feels
all lace and flutter
what he is trying to engender
in the thrashing masses

meanwhile there are children waving
standing
asking
ready to pile on top of the beast
a cow a fish
even immortal boys get splinters
the lives of the saints
are unreliable

## oil moon rises

in a land where peace equals a naked woman
on her knees
milking a goat
where a river of pink babies
is called *the source of life*
I am not a woman at tea
the same as still life with pear
I will not bathe or dance naked
while men in felt hats play cards
I'd rather be a baboon with tongue out
a shock of white snapdragon
amidst bold jungle leaves
gauguin grinds his view
feel his fist in the color
while I want a landscape in pieces
where I can fashion the whole myself
from blue mountains and red roofs
from orchids and a hummingbird
the orchid thought of as refined
a glistening vulva
a girl waiting
flourishes in forest sweat and tangle
with muscle and sinew
tension just under the skin

to keep it from exploding
I don't need your benediction
not for glory
not for your bronze wings
or swirling stumps
my left shoulder glows at dawn
I am the coming storm

## acknowledgments & gratitude

Some of these poems, sometimes in earlier versions, first appeared in the following publications, to whose editors I am grateful: *Anti-, The Bakery, Boston Review, diode poetry journal, elimae, ILK, >kill author, Menacing Hedge, NAP, The Nervous Breakdown, Phoenix in the Jacuzzi, The Offing, Stoked.*

Immense thanks to Bryan Borland and Seth Pennington of Sibling Rivalry Press for their loving support of this project and for being such brilliant lights in the literary landscape.

It's been an unusually hard eighteen months leading up to the finish of this book. I wouldn't have gotten to the other side quite so well without the patient support of the incredible editors of *Vinyl* and YesYes Books and the fierce love offered by Eduardo, Liz, and my brother Matthew.

Deep gratitude to my parents who raised me in a home filled with art and music and literature and conversation, and to Dan and our five children, Kevin, Charles, Nicole, Nick and, in particular, James, who has been my primary reader for the last three years, thank you for your generous hearts.

## notes

Here is a list of the galleries and art spaces I walked through over the past seven years whose collections and architecture influenced the poetry in this book as they offered a conversation with my internal life and occasionally vocabulary from posted descriptions. I am thankful for these spaces and their curators and for the artists whose work lives within their walls and gardens.

Isabella Stewart Gardner Museum
Museum of Fine Arts, Boston
Boston Public Library
Philadelphia Museum of Art
Barnes Foundation, Merion
Barnes Foundation, Philadelphia
Rodin Museum, Philadelphia
San Francisco Museum of Modern Art
The Getty
The Metropolitan Museum of Art
Museum of Modern Art
MOMA PS1
The Cloisters
Portland Art Museum
Lan Su Chinese Garden
Portland Japanese Garden
Seattle Art Museum
RISD Museum
Smithsonian National Gallery of Art
Hirschhorn Museum and Sculpture Gallery
United States Botanical Garden
Arthur M. Sackler Gallery

Freer Gallery of Art
Old Library of Trinity College, Dublin
Christ Church Cathedral, Dublin
St.Patrick's Cathedral, Dublin
The British Museum
The National Gallery, London
Victoria and Albert Museum
Tate Modern
Churchill War Rooms
Westminster Abbey
St Margaret's Church
Van Gogh Museum, Amsterdam
Rijksmuseum
Moco Museum
Louvre
Centre Pompidou
Musée National Picasso
Musée Rodin
Musée d'Orsáy
Notre-Dame de Paris
Sainte-Chapell
Museu Picasso, Barcelona
Museu National d'Art de Catalunya
Sagrada Familia
Casa Batiló
Casa Mila
Museu d'Historia de la Ciutat
Monasterio De Los Jeronimos
Museo Calouste Gulbenkian
Oceanário de Lisboa
Castelo dos Mouros
Palacio Nacional de Sintra

## about the poet

KMA Sullivan is the author of two poetry collections: *Inclined to Riot* (Sibling Rivalry Press, 2019) and *Necessary Fire*, winner of the St. Lawrence Book Award (Black Lawrence Press, 2015). Her poems and essays have appeared in *Boston Review*, *Southern Humanities Review*, *diode*, *The Rumpus*, *Forklift, Ohio*, *The Nervous Breakdown*, *Gertrude*, and elsewhere. She has been awarded residencies in creative nonfiction and poetry at Virginia Center for Creative Arts, Vermont Studio Center, and Summer Literary Seminars. KMA is coeditor in chief of *Vinyl* and the founder and publisher of YesYes Books.

## about the press

Sibling Rivalry Press is an independent press based in Little Rock, Arkansas. It is a sponsored project of Fractured Atlas, a nonprofit arts service organization. Contributions to support the operations of Sibling Rivalry Press are tax-deductible to the extent permitted by law, and your donations will directly assist in the publication of work that disturbs and enraptures. To contribute to the publication of more books like this one, please visit our website and click *donate*.

Sibling Rivalry Press gratefully acknowledges the following donors, without whom this book would not be possible:

| | |
|---|---|
| Tony Taylor | Russell Bunge |
| Mollie Lacy | Joe Pan & Brooklyn Arts Press |
| Karline Tierney | Carl Lavigne |
| Maureen Seaton | Karen Hayes |
| Travis Lau | J. Andrew Goodman |
| Michael Broder & Indolent Books | Diane Greene |
| Robert Petersen | W. Stephen Breedlove |
| Jennifer Armour | Ed Madden |
| Alana Smoot | Rob Jacques |
| Paul Romero | Erik Schuckers |
| Julie R. Enszer | Sugar le Fae |
| Clayton Blackstock | John Bateman |
| Tess Wilmans-Higgins & Jeff Higgins | Elizabeth Ahl |
| Sarah Browning | Risa Denenberg |
| Tina Bradley | Ron Mohring & Seven Kitchens Press |
| Kai Coggin | Guy Choate & Argenta Reading Series |
| Queer Arts Arkansas | Guy Traiber |
| Jim Cory | Don Cellini |
| Craig Cotter | John Bateman |
| Hugh Tipping | Gustavo Hernandez |
| Mark Ward | Anonymous (12) |

9 781943 977581